AUSTRIA

A PICTURE BOOK TO REMEMBER HER BY

Designed by
DAVID GIBBON

Produced by
TED SMART

CRESCENT

INTRODUCTION

Austria is a land with a great and glorious past. In 1278 what may be said to have begun in 800 as the Holy Roman Empire of the German nation was awarded to the Austrian House of Habsburg and became primarily by a process of carefully planned marriages, one of the greatest sovereign dynasties of Europe. For 640 years the Habsburgs presided over a polyglot nation containing at different times, parts or all of what is today Poland, Czechoslovakia, Hungary, the Ukraine, Rumania, Yugoslavia and Italy. Austria as it is now, emerged in 1919 from the collapse of the Austro-Hungarian Empire, of which it had become the heart, only to be subjected to a quarter century of social and economic turbulence, including a Nazi dictatorship. Turmoil and depression followed the at least ostensibly gracious pre-war days of Franz Joseph and it is not surprising if even today, the present pales into insignificance in the light of a nostalgic image of the glittering era of Imperial balls or of the 18th century golden age of cultural expansion under the matriarchal figure of Maria Theresa.

Culture has always played a vital role in the lives of the Austrians. From the days of the earliest Minnesingers, when Walther von der Vogelweide first recited his poignant lyrics before the 12th century Babenburg courts, they have known how to appreciate and encourage the arts. In painting Austria possesses a rich artistic heritage ranging from Romanesque frescoes in the Cathedral at Gurk to the Viennese school of Fantastic Realism, Austrian literature has enriched the world with the works of men such as Grillparzer, Stifter and Hofmannsthal, but above all Austria is a land of music. In the 15th century Maximilian I created a court orchestra and soon every overlord had not only his own orchestra but also his own composer. So began the long tradition whereby so many prominent musicians, among them Glück, Beethoven, Schubert and innumerable others became closely associated with Austria in general and Vienna in particular. The garret rooms of Vienna's gracious buildings have resounded with the attempts of music students aspiring to every conceivable musical height…be it lead tenor in one of Wagner's most grandiose operas or percussion player for the Vienna Philharmonic's New Year's Day concert. Vienna is the domain of the Waltz King Johann Strauss, the composer whose intoxicating melodies caught the ears of the world with their insouciant stories of the gaiety and the beauty of the once pleasure-crazed capital and of the dramatic Austrian countryside.

The music of Strauss was written for a dancing city in which all kinds of extravagancies and fantasies flourished in a glittering whirl of court balls and a hundred other colourful gatherings which ousted more serious considerations from the inebriated minds of its citizens. Today these considerations are perhaps less easily banished but the cultural tradition persists. Vienna's art galleries are still among the most famous in Europe. The Burgtheater considered to be the best German speaking theatre in the 19th century, still ranks among the foremost German stages. The State Opera, completely rebuilt after the war is acclaimed throughout the world and every year the greatest musicians, conductors, singers and instrumentalists flock to Salzburg for the festival. Music still finds its expression in every walk of life…from the meticulously costumed operatic soprano to the corpulent figure in squeaking 'Lederhosen' entertaining 'Heuriger' guests with his zither music, from the carefully disciplined Vienna Boys' Choir performing a Mozart mass in the Hofburg Chapel to the Alpine yodlers who burst into spontaneous song in the streets of a Tyrolean village.

Performances of a more formal nature also provide an opportunity to express that sense of occasion, so essential to a people who have not forgotten their Imperial past. To visit any of the many concert halls is to enter a treasure store of evening dresses, minks and diamonds and to be confronted by a baffling display of circumspect ritual…ritual which makes a title an essential part of any individual's self esteem and so transforms a junior diplomat into 'Ambassador Extraordinary and Plenipotentiary' and a lecturer into 'His Magnificence the University Professor'. The ceremony may take place anywhere…a kiss of the hand is still the normal mode of greeting between men and women who meet in the street…for somehow an appropriate setting is always to hand: outside the magnificent Habsburg Palace of Schönbrunn, in the narrow covered walks of the old town of Innsbruck, before the Hohensalzburg fortress in Salzburg or simply in the precincts of some small baroque church.

Architecture in Austria means in general baroque. From the aftermath of the plague of 1679, which filled the streets with mounds of unburied corpses, there arose a new flamboyant art form. Life assumed the quality of a dream, the extravagant dream of baroque with its gilded saints and cherubs, its soaring twisted columns, its painted heavens on the ceiling and its glorious patinated domes. Austria, it may be suggested, has never really departed from this dream.

At its worst nostalgia for the past is the evasion of the realities of the present (and it is perhaps not altogether insignificant that Vienna, the celebrated 'City of my dreams' was also the city of Freud). Yet Austria does have an identity in the modern world. The establishment of permanent neutrality in 1955 associated with the withdrawal of the four-power troops that had occupied the country for a decade enabled Austria to develop into a stable and socially progressive nation. It forms the vital centre of European traffic between east and west along the great Danubian trade route and between north and south through the spectacular snow-covered mountain passes. Graz forms the gateway to the Balkans, Klagenfurt lies astride important routes to Italy and Yugoslavia and the Linz of the 1970s has become an important industrial centre. Above all a land of such great natural beauty…of the crystal clear lakes of the Salzkammergut and the snow-capped mountains of the Tyrol…holds an irresistible appeal for a flourishing tourist trade. Those who visit Austria are attracted both by the reality and by the dream. There will always be those who protest that the Danube is not blue but muddy grey but they are few by comparison to the thousands who climb into horse-drawn carriages and view the legacies of Imperial prosperity to the accompaniment of Strauss waltzes resounding from the city parks.

Sunlight shimmers on the undisturbed snow and frosted waters of Vorarlberg *left.*

In the northeastern corner of Austria, on the River Danube, lies Vienna, the least spoiled of all the great European capitals… an Imperial city of gracious public buildings, royal palaces and parks. Beyond the famous Burgtheater *above* the skyline is still dominated by the spire of St Stephen's Cathedral (1433) and between the Burgtheater and the Heldenplatz, the Volksgarten *left* still provides a place of quiet refuge. The origins of Schönbrunn *right and above left* date back to the 14th century. The present building however, was begun by Leopold I to the plans of Fischer von Erlach and completed under Maria Theresa as an Imperial residence, which remains resplendent today with many of its original furnishings.

'Hunters in the Snow' *overleaf* by Pieter Brueghel the elder is one of a collection of masterpieces in the Kunsthistorisches Museum.

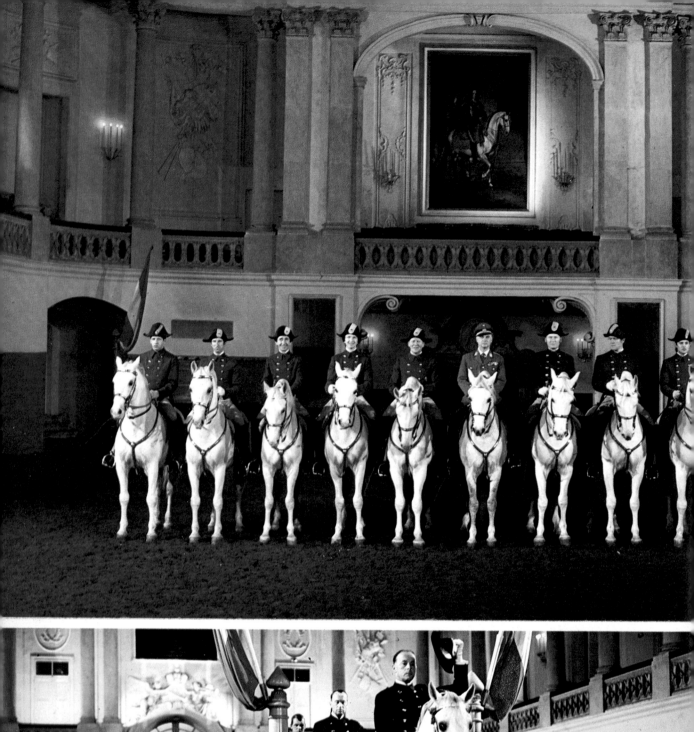

Vienna's Spanish Riding School *on these pages*, with its beautiful baroque riding hall surrounded by a gallery supported by elegant colonnades was designed by Fischer von Erlach. For almost 300 years this hall has been used for displays of the classical Spanish 'haute école' by the famous Lipizzaner horses, which originated in Lipizza (now Lipica in Slovania) in 1580. The style was developed in Vienna by de Plunivel, riding master to Louis XIII of France, to achieve the execution of all the horse's paces and jumps to the highest standard of perfection, and has remained almost unchanged to this day.

From the vine-covered slopes that border Austria's rivers and lakes *below* spring fairy-tale castles and churches. Schönbühel Castle *above*, built in 1820 in neo-classical style with a five-storey tower, is poised on a 130ft high crag rising sheer from the River Danube. Melk *left*, with its Benedictine monastery, one of the most magnificent baroque structures in the world, overlooks the right bank of the Danube like a mighty gateway to the Wachau and at the north end of the Wachau lies the lovely old wine town of Krems *right*. The old mining village of Hallstatt built in terraces on the hillside is a picturesque huddle of houses mirrored in the dark water of the Hallstättersee *overleaf*.

Two thirds of Austria are covered by the snowy peaks of the Eastern Alps punctuated by the crystal clear waters of 66 lakes. On the banks of the Wolfgangsee lie St Gilgen *right*, the picturesque birthplace of Mozart's mother and St Wolfgang itself *above right and below*, site of the celebrated 'White Horse Inn' immortalized in Benatzky's colourful operetta. Near Filzmoos *left*, the Bischofsmütze rises in the shape of a mitre to a height of 8058ft, the spectacular Kitzbüheler Horn *above* overshadows the attractive Tyrolean houses of St Johann in Tirol and not far from it, Ellmau *overleaf* nestles beneath a blanket of snow.

On the banks of the Salzach, Salzburg *on these pages and overleaf* represents a unique combination of scenic Alpine landscape and architectural richness, a blending of the magnificence of baroque and the fine simplicity of the local style that has labelled it one of the world's most beautiful cities. In what was once the seat of the ecclesiastical principality of the Archbishops of Salzburg, who in 1278 were acknowledged as princes of the Holy Roman Empire, the Hohensalzburg fortress *above*, built by Archbishop Gebhard in 1077, still dominates the town from the Mönchsberg and the present cathedral *below and right* was the first church constructed in the Italian style north of the Alps.

In days gone by the Tyrol on *these pages* was known simply as 'the land of the mountains' and this name in itself serves to conjure up the grandeur of its scenery. Here the soaring steeples of tiny village churches are dwarfed by a landscape of deeply indented valleys, green Alpine meadows, precipitous pine covered slopes and jagged mountain peaks.

For many years now Austrian skiing has had a world-wide reputation. In terms of achievement and organisation Austria is one of the leading skiing countries but its snow-covered slopes provide the opportunity not only to improve sporting competence but also to appreciate the magical beauty of mountains like the Kitzsteinhorn *above and overleaf* in winter.

Kitzbühel *below left,* an old-established mountain township made up of characteristic houses with overhanging gable roofs, is a winter sports centre of international renown, surrounded by the breathtaking beauty of the Kitzbüheler Alps *on these pages.* Fieberbrunn *above,* set among these spectacular mountains, is also famous for its sulphur baths and derives its name from the fact that in 1534 Countess Margarete Maultasch was cured of fever here.

In the early days of skiing only one stick was used and stiff hats, impractical trousers or long skirts restricted rapid movement. Today tremendous developments in the sport have led to a constant quest for improved amenities. Cable cars, chair lifts and ski-tows have opened up the finest areas to visitors without the necessity for an arduous ascent and the latest technical achievements have been made available to skiers. Hochsölden *overleaf* is just one of a multitude of high altitude resorts offering every possible luxury.

Hand in hand with the timeless beauty of such natural landscapes as the Biberkopf mountain *above right*, Berwang *right* or the green waters of the Fernsteinsee *left*, goes a love of tradition. A village band assembles *below* in traditional Tyrolean dress and Kirchberg *overleaf* is renowned for its ancient custom of processing in a 'Pardon Ride' to the historic Schwedenkapelle at Corpus Christi. Near Seefeld, the village church in Mosern *above* overlooks the spectacular Inn valley.

Characteristic timber houses in Alpbach *above and right* blend harmoniously into the surrounding pasture-land and in the famous Zillertal *left and below,* flowers blossom on the lower slopes of gorges which run upwards into regions of perennial snow. Pertisau *overleaf* lies on the banks of the Achensee, one of Austria's most enchanting lakes.

The villages and towns near the Zillertal, which in spring and summer are lost in fields of Alpine flowers, are transformed in winter by the delicate traceries of frost and snow. At the heart of the Zillertal Alps themselves *right* lies a region of magnificent glaciers.

Innsbruck *above* is the capital of the Tyrol with a history which extends over 700 years. Its particular attraction lies in its extraordinarily beautiful situation at the foot of the Nordkette of the Karwendel mountains. Innsbruck's heart is the Maria-Theresien Strasse *left* with its famous view of the steep faces of the Nordkette and Cristoforo Benedetti's 'St Anne's Column', a very characteristic example of the baroque style. *Below,* trees and blossoms overhang a pool in the city park. The sun sets *right* over the Inn Valley and Zirl *overleaf* huddles at the foot of fir-covered slopes.

During the winter months a special beauty is derived from the contrast between the villages, each with its own small church in an idyllic setting of clusters of larch and fir trees and the rugged snow-covered mountains which tower above them. Those who flock to the ski-slopes are attracted not only by the skiing but also by the opportunity to admire this beauty and to bask in the sun's rays reflected off the snow.

The texture and colouring of the scenes *on these pages* provide an excellent illustration of why Austria's infinite variety of churches, mountain ranges and rivers have been a source of inspiration to countless artists. *Above left and above* Nassereith, *below left* Lermoos, *below* the Mieminger mountains and *right* Heiterwang. The Brenner Autobahn *overleaf* wends its way along an old Roman route to the Austrian and Italian frontier 4495ft up in the Brenner Pass.

The Tyrol is scattered with a multitude of towns and villages with their own distinctive atmospheres and points of interest. Seefeld *right,* with its beautiful little church *above,* is a particularly popular winter sports centre and Igls *above left* is another very attractive ski resort at the foot of the magnificent Patscherkofel. Sölden *below left* marks the beginning of the upper Ötztal, the longest side valley of the Inn and Ober-Gurgl *below right,* set at a height of 6325ft in the Ötztal Alps, is the highest village with a church in the whole of Austria.

Art develops naturally in this framework of natural beauty and many of these villages have given birth to artists of outstanding talent. Nauders *left* was the birthplace both of the famous painter, Karl Blaas and the blind sculptor, Kleinhans. A strong artistic sense is still rooted in the mountain people and the Gothic parish church in Schönberg *below,* with its baroque altar and rococo choirstalls, bears witness to the kind of craftsmanship that may still be found throughout Austria.
Overleaf: At the foot of the Omeshorn, its lights twinkling in the snow, lies Lech am Arlberg with its early Gothic church crowned by a massive and striking tower.

Holzgau *above left*, with its
meticulously decorated houses, huddles
in the Lechtal near the boundary
between the Tyrol and Vorarlberg, the
most westerly province of Austria.
Vorarlberg has become to a large extent
industrial but modern developments
have not spoiled the dramatic
countryside which surrounds
picturesque villages like Schröcken
above or Wörth *left*, or detracted from
the popularity of its ski centres *right*.

It was on the slopes of St Anton,
Arlberg *far right* that at the beginning
of the century Hannes Schneider
initiated his famous Alpine skiing
technique.

At the foot of the Grossglockner,
Austria's highest mountain,
Heiligenblut *overleaf* clusters round
the characteristic bell-tower of its late
15th century church.

Pages 62 and 63: From a mighty crag
above Kufstein, Geroldseck Castle
presides over one of the most important
and prosperous Tyrolean towns.

First published in Great Britain 1979 by Colour Library International Ltd.
© Illustrations: Colour Library International Ltd, 163 East 64th Street, New York 10021.
Vienna photographs: © Foto UFVW-Markowitszh
Colour separations by Fercrom, Barcelona, Spain.
Display and text filmsetting by Focus Photoset, London, England.
Printed and bound by SAGDOS - Brugherio (MI), Italy.
Published by Crescent Books, a division of Crown Publishers Inc.
Library of Congress Catalogue Card No. 79-87536
CRESCENT 1979